How to be a Coffee Bean

How to be a Coffee Bean

111 LIFE-CHANGING WAYS TO CREATE POSITIVE CHANGE

JON GORDON

Bestselling Author of
The Energy Bus

DAMON WEST

Bestselling Coauthor of
The Coffee Bean

WILEY

Library of Congress Cataloging-in-Publication Data is Available:
ISBN 9781119430285 (Hardback)
ISBN 9781119430629 (ePub)
ISBN 9781119430773 (ePDF)

Cover Design: Paul McCarthy
Cover Image: © Getty Images/Kim Thoa Vo/EyeEm
SKY10037310_120822

Contents

HOW TO BE A COFFEE BEAN

HOW TO BE A COFFEE BEAN

Prologue: The Origin Story of *The Coffee Bean*

If you've read *The Coffee Bean*, you know it's a short book with a powerful message: a simple lesson about the power to transform your world from the inside out.

You may have even heard that I was first introduced to the story of the coffee bean in the summer of 2009, while I was in Dallas County Jail. I was awaiting transfer to a Texas maximum-security prison to serve a life sentence for organized crime and was filled with overwhelming fear of the unknown, when another inmate shared it with me. He used the example of prison as the pot of boiling water, illustrating the three options I had: be like the carrot, which turns soft; be like the egg, which turns hard; or be like the coffee bean, which transforms the water into coffee. He told me that the power was inside me, and I believed him.

What you may not know is how *The Coffee Bean* book came to be, exactly 10 years later, in the summer of 2019. Well, the back story actually starts in 2010, when Chad Morris walked into a bookstore in Destin, Florida. At the time, he had just left a successful career as a Texas high school football coach to take a job as offensive coordinator for the University of Tulsa football team.

That day, while on vacation, he was looking for a good book to read with his quarterbacks. Immediately, a book caught his eye because it had a whistle on the cover. This spoke to him as a coach, so he grabbed Jon Gordon's *Training Camp: What the Best Do Better Than Everyone Else* off the shelf and read the entire book on the beach that day!

Satisfied that he had found the perfect book, Chad purchased copies for all of his quarterbacks. The pages of *Training Camp* contributed to a great season at Tulsa. In fact, after one season in college football, Chad's offensive coaching skills got the attention of one of the youngest head coaches in college football: Dabo Swinney. Recognizing Chad's talent, Dabo hired him to fill their newly vacant offensive coordinator coaching position.

As soon as Chad was settled in at Clemson, he walked into Dabo's office one afternoon in 2011, with a copy of *Training Camp* in his hand. He gave the book to Dabo and told him how impactful it was at Tulsa and that he felt it could be just as impactful for the culture at Clemson.

From time to time, Chad would ask Dabo if he had had a chance to read *Training Camp*. Dabo assured Chad he would read it before their own training camp began in August.

In June, Chad and his family were again in Destin, Florida, on their annual vacation. He was relaxing and soaking up the rays on the beach when his cell phone rang. It was Dabo calling.

Chad sat up in his beach chair, ready to talk offensive strategy with his head coach. But Dabo wasn't calling to discuss Xs and Os; he was calling to tell Chad he had just finished *Training Camp*. Dabo agreed that the book would work well with the culture they were building at Clemson.

That 2011 season, Clemson used *Training Camp* as the team read, and the team subsequently won 10 games.

In the fall training camp of 2012, Clemson used *The Energy Bus* as their team read and Jon Gordon spoke to the Clemson Tigers for the

HOW TO BE A COFFEE BEAN

first time. As Clemson's culture of winning began to take root and grow, Jon was a consistent presence at every training camp. His books became team reads and his principles became their principles. On a personal level, Dabo and Jon began a close friendship, which eventually saw both of Jon's kids going to Clemson for their education.

* * *

While Dabo was bringing Jon in every year to positively impact his teams, I was using the coffee bean message to change that maximum-security prison into a pot of coffee. In fact, my transformation into a servant leader, and the transformation of the prison's culture, was so extreme, the parole board released me from prison in 2015, with the instruction to *find more coffee beans in society*.

That's exactly what I did. I started sharing the coffee bean message all over my little area of southeast Texas. As the message was taking root, I dreamed of sharing it with college football teams because I had once played college football. I felt my back story and the message of the coffee bean could be especially useful to student athletes. Until that opportunity presented itself, I continued to get in "reps" every chance I got, sharing the message with any audience who would have me.

One such opportunity came in January 2017, in Houston, Texas. A friend of mine, Michael Orta, invited me to the Bear Bryant Coach of the Year Award, where the best college football coach in America would be named. I felt so out of place at the Toyota Center that night. One by one, I met each head coach and gave them my awkward and untested elevator pitch.

And, one by one, each coach passed on my offer. After being rejected in the first hour by all but one coach there, I was in the corner of the Toyota Center licking my wounds and feeling sorry for myself. The voice in my head said, *Go home. Quit. That last coach is going to tell you what you already know, like all the others.*

xiii

But I could not quit because, as a coffee bean, I was constitutionally incapable of quitting.

So I stalked that last coach around the room that night until was I finally in front of him. Dabo Swinney listened to my pitch and asked me if I had a card on me. I gave him my card and he hurried away. Defeated and exhausted, I was relieved it was finally over. I had been rejected by every coach there that night, but I felt good because I left it all on the field. Being a coffee bean means that you don't have to win all your fights, but you must fight all your fights.

A few months later, I received an email from Michael Dooley, director of football operations at Clemson. He mentioned that Coach Swinney had met me at an award show in Houston and that he would love to have me speak to his team. "Do you have August 1 open?" he asked.

Was he kidding? I had the first of every month open!

In August 2017, seven months after I met Dabo in Houston, I shared the coffee bean message with the Clemson Tigers. After that presentation, Dabo believed in the coffee bean so much that he started calling other head coaches in college football—beginning with Nick Saban—to bring me in to speak to their teams. As the other coaches began bringing me in, the message grew.

In August 2018, the coffee bean message was launched on a rocket ship, when Jon Gordon called me out of the blue. He told me he had just spoken to Dabo's team and that Dabo pulled him aside to tell him my story and about the coffee bean message.

I said to Jon, "That's really cool that Dabo still talks about the coffee bean. He said he uses it in their culture at Clemson."

Jon got to the point. He told me, "Damon, the coffee bean message is powerful. Let's team up to write a book. We'll call it *The Coffee Bean*. The world needs this message."

My jaw dropped. This was different than a coach calling me to speak to their team. Jon Gordon had just asked me to coauthor a book. I fumbled for the correct response, saying, "Wow! Jon, I'm speechless, humbled that you're asking me to write this book with you. . .but the truth is you don't need me. You should write the book yourself."

"That won't work," Jon said, with conviction in his voice. "I always listen to what God tells me, and God told me to write this book with you. I could immediately envision it when Dabo was telling me about this incredible message. Let's write this book together, Damon. *The world needs the coffee bean message!*"

* * *

Imagine if Chad Morris had never walked into that Destin bookstore in 2010, or if he had chosen any other book to read with his team. Imagine if Jon had never visited Clemson. Imagine if I had left that awards show without meeting Dabo. Imagine if Dabo hadn't told Jon about my story and the coffee bean message.

There would be no coffee bean. And this book you are reading would not exist.

The Coffee Bean was meant to be, and you were meant to be a coffee bean. That's why Jon and I wrote this book.

So now you know the back story.

Our goal is to help you create positivity in your life and write the story of your life. You may have read the life-changing allegory of *The Coffee Bean,* but now we want to equip you with the strategies and principles to become a coffee bean.

Let's get started.

—Damon West

How to be a Coffee Bean

2

HOW TO BE A COFFEE BEAN

1

Create from the Inside Out, Not the Outside In

Don't let the environment or situation transform you. As the coffee bean, you have the power inside you to transform your environment. Don't let your circumstance define you. You define your circumstance with your attitude, energy, and actions.

HOW TO BE A COFFEE BEAN

2

Be a Big Dose of Vitamin C, Instead of a Germ

Your energy is contagious, and every day you have a choice to affect people with your positive energy or infect people with your negative energy. You can be a germ, or you can be Vitamin C. Decide to be Vitamin C.

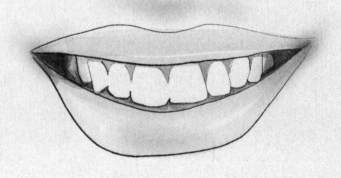

HOW TO BE A COFFEE BEAN

3

Smile

Did you know that when you smile your brain produces serotonin, which is an antidepressant? And when you smile at someone, they produce more serotonin in their brain as well. Just by smiling at someone, you're helping them and helping yourself. So, whatever your job is, remember, you're also a pharmacist.

HOW TO BE A COFFEE BEAN

4

Neutralize Energy Vampires

Energy vampires suck the positive energy out of individuals, teams, and organizations. Your positive energy must be greater than their negativity. Don't let them bring you down. Instead, lift others up.

9

10

HOW TO BE A COFFEE BEAN

5

Be a Thermostat, Not a Thermometer

A thermostat sets and creates the temperature in the room. The thermometer measures it. When you are a thermometer, you let others be the thermostat, and how you are measured is defined by them. When you decide to be a thermostat, you create the energy and atmosphere in the room. Your body language and positive energy can change the energy everywhere you go and create the atmosphere.

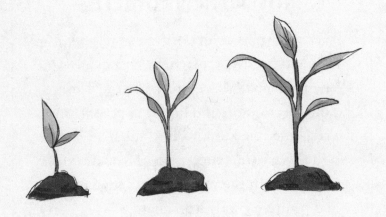

HOW TO BE A COFFEE BEAN

6

Turn Challenges into Opportunities

Every challenge is an opportunity to learn, grow, and improve. When faced with a challenge, ask, "What can I learn from this?" "How can I improve and grow?" "What do I want now and what actions do I need to take?" When you do this, your challenges lead to you adapting, innovating, learning, and growing.

HOW TO BE A COFFEE BEAN

7

Learn from Failure

Too many people let failure bring them down. They see it as a definition of who they are, and this sabotages their self-esteem and identity. Instead of changing the world, they feel sorry for themselves. We want you to realize that failure is not meant to define you. It's meant to refine you to be all you are meant to be so you can make a greater difference in the world.

HOW TO BE A COFFEE BEAN

8

Take Accountability and Make Amends

Everyone makes mistakes. It's part of being human. In fact, making mistakes is often how we learn to do things correctly. Accepting that we made a mistake is only half of the process of owning our behaviors. Taking accountability is the other half. It means that we make amends for our mistakes and transgressions that affect others, and we do not make excuses for our behaviors.

18

HOW TO BE A COFFEE BEAN

9

Live in the Moment

Your energy is greatest in the present moment. Daydreaming about the future or dwelling on the past causes you to think about a different time and moment than the one you are living in. When this happens, your energy is divided and weaker. When you live in the present moment, your energy is the greatest, and you are your most powerful and impactful self.

19

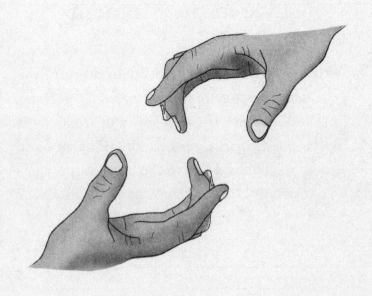

20

HOW TO BE A COFFEE BEAN

10

Practice Servant Leadership

The secret to life is servant leadership. Servant leadership is about committing your time and energy to help others. It requires you to be selfless and put the needs of others before your own. Look for ways to serve others today, and you'll be demonstrating leadership.

21

22

HOW TO BE A COFFEE BEAN

11

Encourage Others

Coffee beans are always looking for ways to encourage others. The word "encourage" literally means to put courage into. When you encourage someone, you put courage into them, and you bring out the best in them. We all need encouragement from time to time. That's why it's so important to tell people things like "Great job," "You've got this," and "I believe in you."

HOW TO BE A COFFEE BEAN

12

Work out Mentally Each Day

You are not only what you eat. You are also what you consume in your mind. Every book you read, the websites you frequent, the social media accounts you follow, the shows you watch, and the people you communicate with fill your mind with positivity or negativity. Feed your mind and soul well by choosing positive mental food.

HOW TO BE A COFFEE BEAN

13

Take a Thank You Walk

It's impossible to be grateful and stressed at the
same time. Make the time each day to go for
a walk. On this walk, think about what you are
grateful for. You can even say these things out
loud. When you are feeling blessed, you can't
be stressed.

27

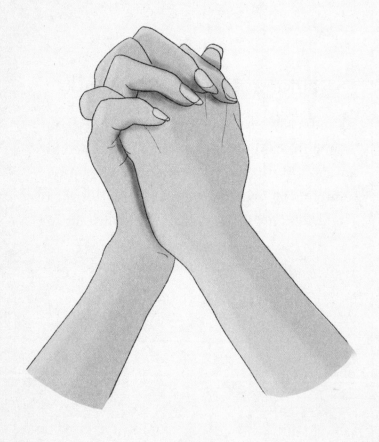

HOW TO BE A COFFEE BEAN

14

Live with Faith, Not Fear

What do fear and faith have in common besides beginning with the letter "F"? They both believe in futures that have not happened yet. Fear believes in a negative future, and faith believes in a positive future. If neither has happened yet, why wouldn't you choose to believe in a positive future? Choose to believe in a positive future.

HOW TO BE A COFFEE BEAN

15

Have a "Get to" Mindset

Remind yourself each day that you don't *have* to do anything; rather, you *get* to do something. This simple shift in your daily outlook will change your perspective.

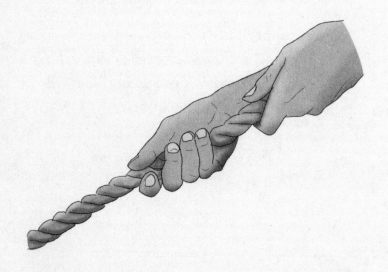

HOW TO BE A COFFEE BEAN

16

Help Someone Be Successful

You aren't a true success unless you help others be successful. And here's the great thing about helping others improve and grow. When you help others improve, you improve. When you help others grow, you grow.

HOW TO BE A COFFEE BEAN

17

Shout Praise and Whisper Criticism

Let everyone know how great someone is, but quietly criticize someone individually in order to help them get better. This makes you a positive communicator and makes others better.

35

HOW TO BE A COFFEE BEAN

18

Don't Be Bitter, Get Better

It's easy to let past events hold you back and weigh you down with bitterness and anger. Coffee beans don't let past circumstances make them worse. They focus on getting better and creating a positive future.

HOW TO BE A COFFEE BEAN

Be Great Today

Don't worry about your greatness in the future. Just focus on being your best today. If you do this each day, you will create greatness.

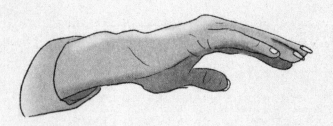

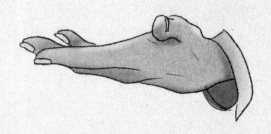

20

Control What
You Can Control

There is a lot in life you can't control. The key is
to focus on what you can control: your attitude,
effort, and actions.

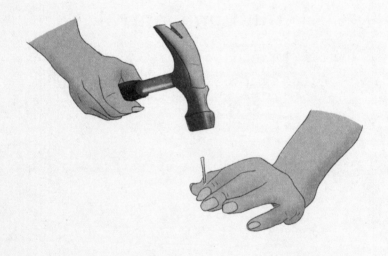

42

HOW TO BE A COFFEE BEAN

21

Put in the Work

If you want something you've never had, you must be willing to do things you've never done. Simply put, you must put in the work. Whatever your hopes, goals, and dreams are, it is up to you to do what it takes to make them a reality.

43

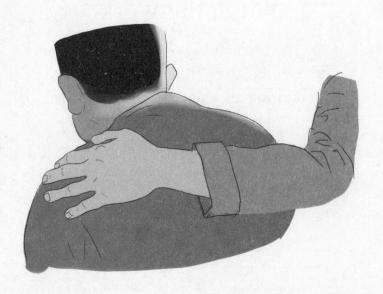

44

HOW TO BE A COFFEE BEAN

Care More

When you care more, you stand out in a world
where most don't seem to care anymore.
When you care, you do more, give more,
and help others become more.

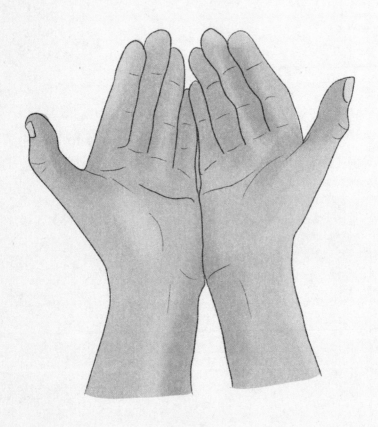

HOW TO BE A COFFEE BEAN

23

Be Vulnerable

Vulnerability is a strength, and vulnerable people let their guards down and invite others in to connect with them in a deeper, more meaningful way. People will be impressed by your accomplishments, but they will trust you when you reveal your flaws and imperfections. When you are vulnerable, you help others be vulnerable too, and this changes the dynamic of relationships and everyone with whom you interact.

47

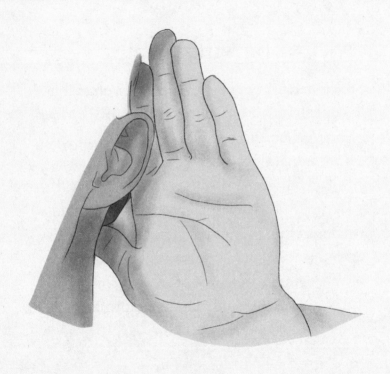

48

HOW TO BE A COFFEE BEAN

24

Be a Great Listener

One of the fundamental truths of
communication is that every person wants
to feel like they have been heard. When you
hear others, and they know you are listening
to them, they will trust you more and want to
follow you. So don't just talk to influence others.
Remember that listening is how you
build a great relationship and earn the right
to speak into someone's life.

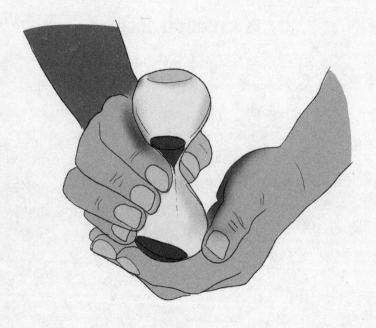

HOW TO BE A COFFEE BEAN

25

Value Time

Once time is gone, it is gone for good, and all the money in the world cannot buy one more second of time. Time is the great equalizer, affecting each person the same way because we each get the same 24 hours in a day. What is not equal, however, is how each person uses their 24 hours. Value time by making the most of the time you have.

52

HOW TO BE A COFFEE BEAN

26

Take a Personal Inventory

A business cannot operate efficiently without taking inventory. In fact, a business will probably go bankrupt if it does not keep track of its inventory. The same thing happens to people who do not regularly take a personal inventory. They become emotionally bankrupt. Take an inventory of your life. What is good in your life? What is nourishing you? What is sabotaging you? What is no longer serving you? What is a waste? What is something you need to add? This will help you take stock of what you have, what you need, and what needs to go.

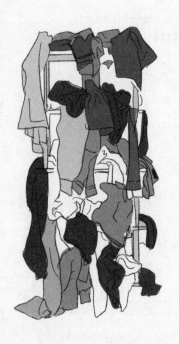

HOW TO BE A COFFEE BEAN

27

Clear the Clutter

When you take your personal inventory, you'll want to identify things that need to go. Just as your home needs a good spring cleaning, you also need to clean up your personal life regularly and take out your trash. When you let go of the things that are wasting your time and energy, you'll be able to make room for new energy and positive things in your life.

56

HOW TO BE A COFFEE BEAN

28

Practice Empathy

Empathy is when we feel with others. It's putting yourself in their shoes and asking yourself, "How would I want someone to treat me if this were happening to me?" Once we feel with others and become aware of their struggles, then we can be the most useful for them and help them.

58

HOW TO BE A COFFEE BEAN

29

Give Without Keeping Score

Coffee beans don't give to get. They give out of love, not obligation. They give from the heart. When you keep score, you both lose. When you give simply to give, you both win.

60

HOW TO BE A COFFEE BEAN

30

Add Value

In every interaction, conversation, project, and workday, look to add value. Make someone better. Share something helpful. Write something that will improve someone's outlook. Give a tip that will impact their bottom line. Look for ways each day to enrich the lives of others. When you add value, you become more valuable to others.

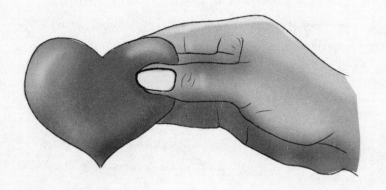

HOW TO BE A COFFEE BEAN

31

Lead with Love, Not an Agenda

In other words, make sharing love your agenda.
People can tell if you have selfish motives,
and when this happens, you lose the power to
lead and influence others. At the core of being
human, we all want to be loved. People will
follow a leader who makes others feel loved.
When you love them, they will follow you.

HOW TO BE A COFFEE BEAN

32

Be a Connector

Coffee beans connect. They look for ways to connect people who would benefit from getting to know each other. The more you connect good people, the more good gets done in the world. As you go through your life, look for opportunities to connect people who would benefit each other and the world by becoming friends.

HOW TO BE A COFFEE BEAN

33

Write Thank You Notes

Pick up a pen and paper (the old-fashioned way of writing) to tell someone how grateful you are for them or what they did for you. The act of writing a thank you note not only makes you happier, it makes the person reading the note happier.

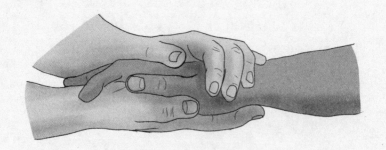

HOW TO BE A COFFEE BEAN

34

Choose to Forgive

It's been said that forgiveness is the ultimate weight loss. When you forgive, you let go of the heavy energy holding you back from becoming all you're meant to be. You let go of your resentments, jealousy, and anger. This doesn't mean you forget. It just means you let go of the burden weighing you down so you can move forward and create a positive future.

69

HOW TO BE A COFFEE BEAN

35

Love Tough

When you love someone, you earn the right
to challenge them to be their best. Tough love
works when love comes first. When people
know you love them, they will let you be tough
with them and make them better.

HOW TO BE A COFFEE BEAN

36

Laugh out Loud

Laughter is not just good for the soul. It's also good for the heart. Research shows that laugher actually improves heart health and happiness. And when you laugh with others or make them laugh, you spread positive contagious energy that makes everyone healthier and happier. Read a joke. Tell a funny story. Share a funny video.

HOW TO BE A COFFEE BEAN

37

Use Your Gifts for a Bigger Purpose

You are not here just for you. You are a part of something bigger than you. The gifts (talent, skill, resources) you have are meant to be shared to enrich the lives of as many people as possible. When you share your gifts with the world, you make yourself and the world better.

76

38

Be Positive, Especially on Difficult Days

Positive doesn't mean Pollyanna. We are positive, not because life is easy. We are positive because life can be hard. It's not about ignoring your current reality. It's about being positive and optimistic in order to create a better reality.

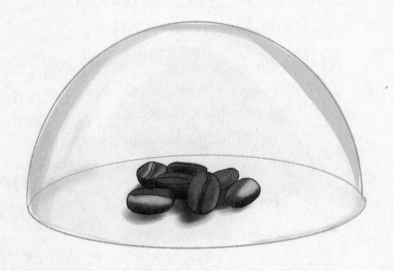

HOW TO BE A COFFEE BEAN

39

Don't Let Negativity Sour Your Situation

Being a coffee bean doesn't mean you sugar-coat your challenging situations in life. It means that you will not let negatives sour your situation. You can acknowledge the situation is difficult while seeking ways and taking action to improve it.

HOW TO BE A COFFEE BEAN

40

Embrace Change

The wave of change is always happening. If you resist the wave of change, it will crush you. But if you embrace change, you will ride the wave and create a positive future. Always remember during times of change, your perspective about change will determine whether you succeed. Embrace it and thrive.

HOW TO BE A COFFEE BEAN

41

Enjoy the Ride

You only have one ride through life, so make sure you enjoy it. This doesn't mean you won't face hard times. It means you will find joy in the journey and do your best to make the most of the life you have been given.

83

HOW TO BE A COFFEE BEAN

42

Look for the Good

What you look for, you will find. When you look for the good, you will find more of it. When you look for what people are doing right, you will find them doing the right things more often.

HOW TO BE A COFFEE BEAN

43

Don't Chase Success

Instead of chasing success, decide to make a difference and success will find you. It's a different approach than what most of the world says, but coffee beans are different. When you make a difference, success will be a by-product of all the great work you do and impact you make.

88

HOW TO BE A COFFEE BEAN

44

Get Excited about Life

People think when you have an exciting life you will get excited about life, but it works the other way. When you get excited about life, you get a life that is exciting.

HOW TO BE A COFFEE BEAN

45

Rise and Shine

Every day you have a choice. You can rise and whine or rise and shine. When you rise and shine, you're able to shine on others and be the coffee bean that you are meant to be.

HOW TO BE A COFFEE BEAN

46

Believe in Miracles

If you don't believe in miracles, remember
that you live on a giant rock hurtling through
outer space at 60,000 mph, spinning 1,000 mph.
Everything about our existence is a miracle and
every day is a miracle. Believe that miracles are
possible, and you will start seeing them as the
result of your positive attitude and actions.

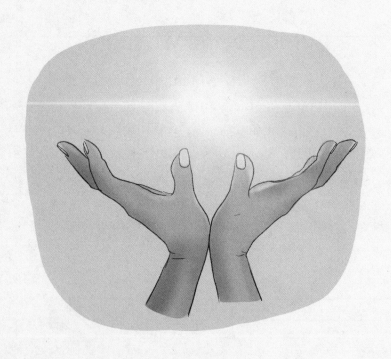

94

HOW TO BE A COFFEE BEAN

47

Remember That
You Are a Miracle

Scientists say that the odds of your existence are the same as taking two million dice that have a trillion sides, rolling them and having them all come out to the same number. The odds of this happening are basically zero. In other words, the fact you were born is a miracle. So today, be the miracle that you are.

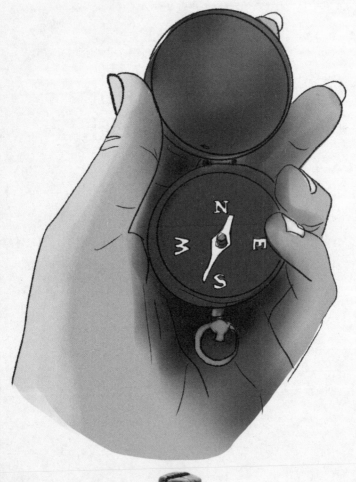

96

HOW TO BE A COFFEE BEAN

48

Don't Seek Happiness

Decide to live with passion and purpose instead.
When you live with passion and purpose,
happiness is a by-product of that. No one
ever finds happiness by seeking it. They find
it when they are living a life of meaning,
purpose, and impact.

97

HOW TO BE A COFFEE BEAN

49

Be Kind

It doesn't cost anything to be kind and yet
it pays dividends in the world. Kindness is
contagious and when you are kind to people,
they will likely be more kind to others.
One kind person can have a ripple effect
that impacts hundreds or even thousands of
people. Remember, kindness is created through
your tone of voice, body language, words,
and actions.

HOW TO BE A COFFEE BEAN

50

Compliment Someone

Everyone wants to feel good about themselves. When you compliment people, you make them feel good, and in turn, they will radiate more positive energy. One sincere compliment can make someone feel like a million bucks and spark a contagious ripple effect of kindness.

101

HOW TO BE A COFFEE BEAN

51

Spread Positive Gossip

Instead of being someone who talks behind people's backs in a negative way, be the person who always talks positively about your friends and family to other people. Talk about the amazing things they're doing and their great characteristics and qualities.

ROOKIE
OF THE
YEAR

HOW TO BE A COFFEE BEAN

52

Think Like a Rookie

The curse of experience can cause you to long for the good ole days and complain about the way things are, become unadaptable to change, and expect rejection or bad outcomes because they happened in the past. Rookies, on the other hand, are not burdened by the past. They believe anything is possible, put their head down, work hard, and create the good ole days right now.

106

HOW TO BE A COFFEE BEAN

53

Be a Possibility Thinker

Too many people focus on what is impossible.
Instead, choose to think about what is possible.
What can you do? What difference can you
make? What is possible if you work hard,
innovate, and create? Believe in what's possible
and you will make it happen.

108

HOW TO BE A COFFEE BEAN

54

Don't Rush the Future

You may want things to happen *now*, but more than likely if you got what you wanted *now*, you wouldn't be ready for it. The process prepares you, strengthens you, shapes you, develops character, and creates success—not in your time, but in the right time.

110

55

Choose Positive Thinking

As Henry Ford said, "Think you can or think you can't. Either way, you're correct." If you think you can, more than likely you will.

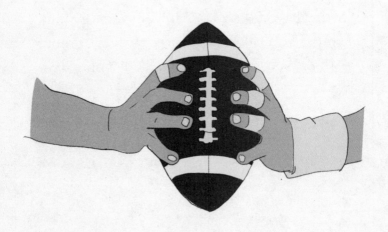

HOW TO BE A COFFEE BEAN

56

Be an Over-Believer

When Dabo Swinney, the head coach of the
University of Clemson football team, was asked
if he was an overachiever, he responded, "No,
I'm an over-believer." He believes it was his
over-belief in what his team could accomplish
that led to several national championships.
When you are an over-believer, you will be
an overachiever.

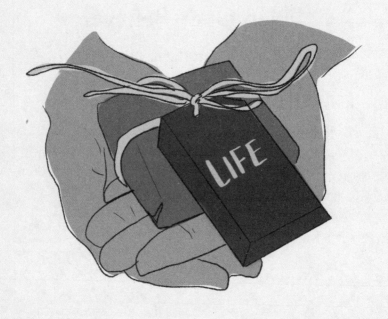

HOW TO BE A COFFEE BEAN

57

See Life as a Gift

Anybody who has had a near-death experience or overcome a serious illness understands how precious life is. It's something you can lose in a moment. That's why you should see life as a gift, not an obligation. It's a gift you get to open each day with wonder, curiosity, joy, and hope.

HOW TO BE A COFFEE BEAN

58

Say Please and Thank You

These two simple phrases go a long way to showing gratitude, humility, and respect. Even if others don't say it, you can always choose to say it and set a standard that others will follow.

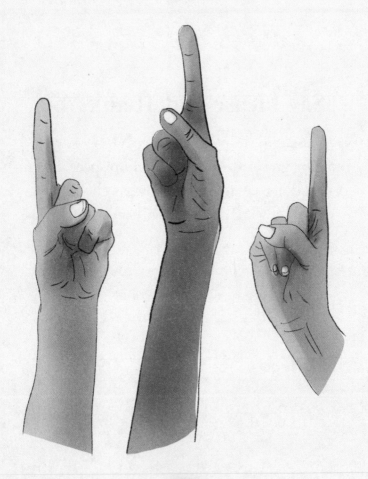

HOW TO BE A COFFEE BEAN

59

Be Demanding, Not Demeaning

To bring out the best in someone you often must demand their best. Don't let them settle for anything but their best effort. Yet in the process of being demanding, make sure you aren't demeaning. Don't put them down. Don't call them out. Call them up to greatness.

120

HOW TO BE A COFFEE BEAN

60

Live with Integrity

Integrity is the number-one factor in building trust and creating success. When people trust you, they want to work with you. Integrity is the result of your words and actions being in alignment. It's as simple as saying what you're going to do and doing what you said.

HOW TO BE A COFFEE BEAN

61

Delete Negativity

You know that delete button on your phone or computer that you hit to remove the last letter or word you just wrote? You can do the same in your life. Delete negative words and phrases from your vocabulary and life. Identify a few negative words you commonly think or say, and delete them today for good.

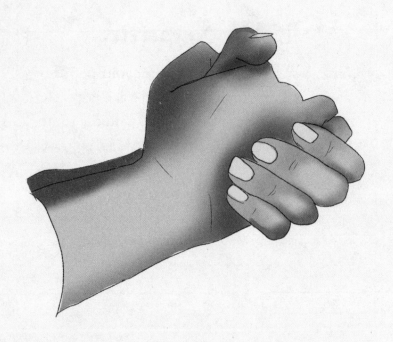

HOW TO BE A COFFEE BEAN

62

Pray and Meditate

Research shows that prayer and meditation boost your mood and your immune system, enhance your mental health and happiness, and lead to greater clarity and more focus. We would also add that it makes you a more positive and powerful force in the world.

125

HOW TO BE A COFFEE BEAN

63

Love the Process

There's no such thing as an overnight success. It often takes 10 years or more to master your craft or achieve success. But if you are patient, keep working, and love the process, you'll love what the process produces.

64

Fuel Your Life with Purpose

Remember why you do what you do. We don't
get burned out because of what we do. We get
burned out because we forget why we do it.
Each day, let your purpose refresh and recharge
you so you can make a greater impact.

129

HOW TO BE A COFFEE BEAN

65

Love. Serve. Care.

If you want to be someone who leads and influences others, start there. Love. Serve. Care. When you love others, serve them, and show you care, you will make a difference and become an amazing leader.

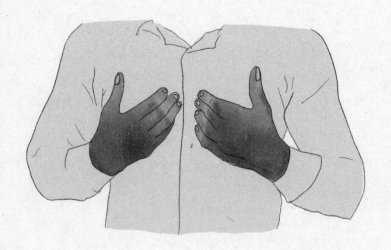

HOW TO BE A COFFEE BEAN

66

Talk to Yourself

Talk to yourself rather than listen to yourself. Instead of listening to your complaints, fears, and doubts, talk to yourself with words of encouragement. This helps you win the battle of your mind and your life.

HOW TO BE A COFFEE BEAN

67

Remember When You Succeeded

When you lose your confidence, remember a time when you overcame adversity to accomplish something. If you did it once, you can do it again. Each night before you go to bed, think about your success of the day.

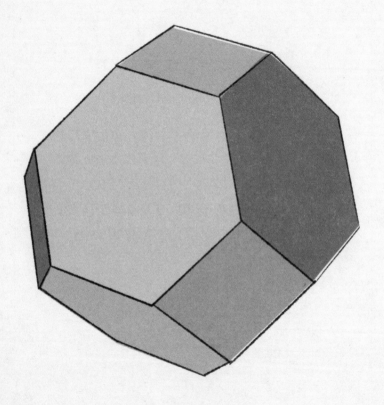

HOW TO BE A COFFEE BEAN

68

Tap into the Power of Perspective

When you are going through a tough time, think about ways it could be worse. Think about those who are worse off than you. Think about how bad things could be. This will help you have a more positive perspective right now.

137

HOW TO BE A COFFEE BEAN

69

Be a Problem Solver

You can be a problem creator or a problem solver. A lot of people create problems, but coffee beans solve them. When you are a problem solver, you will always be needed and valued in a world with a lot of problems.

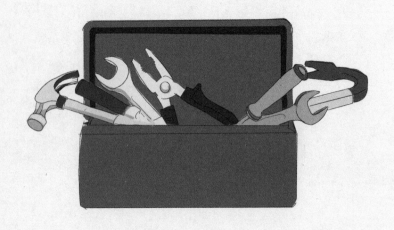

HOW TO BE A COFFEE BEAN

70

Focus on Solutions, Not Complaints

You can complain about it or do something about it. If you're going to complain about something, then be ready to offer a solution. Use complaints as a catalyst to create new innovations, ideas, and better processes. When you want to complain, make it a habit to identify a solution.

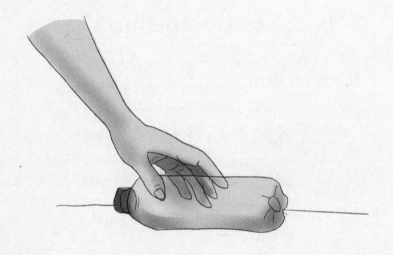

HOW TO BE A COFFEE BEAN

71

Leave a Place Better than You Found It

Wherever you go, make people and places better because you were there. Make the place brighter. Make the people more hopeful.

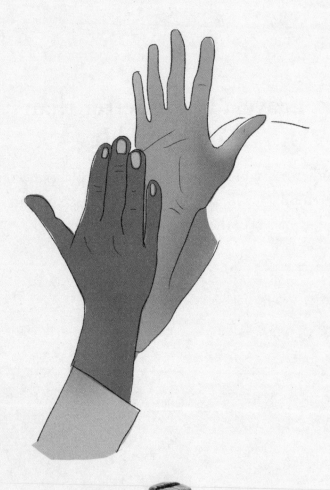

HOW TO BE A COFFEE BEAN

Be a Great Team Member

Your team doesn't care if you're a superstar.
They care if you're a super-teammate.
Look for ways to serve the team and make
the team better.

145

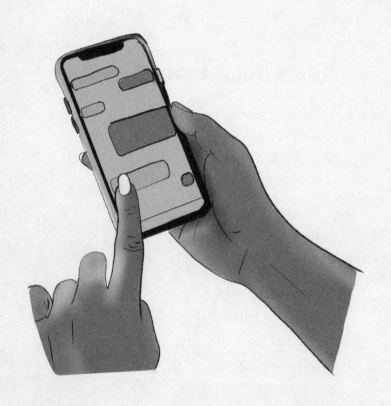

146

HOW TO BE A COFFEE BEAN

73

Communicate Responsively

Return your calls, texts, and emails in a timely manner—even if it's just to respond that you saw their message and will get back to them. If you don't respond, people may feel like you're ignoring them. Where there's a void in communication, negativity will fill it. So make sure you fill the void.

148

HOW TO BE A COFFEE BEAN

74

Build a Great Team

No one creates success alone. We all need a team to be successful. Surround yourself with supportive people and other coffee beans who want to make a positive difference with you.

HOW TO BE A COFFEE BEAN

75

Wake up Unplugged

When you wake up in the morning, give yourself 30 minutes before checking your phone, social media, or email. When you get your mind right, your day will go all right.

I AM HERE TO MAKE A DIFFERENCE

I AM!

I AM A COFFEE BEAN

I AM MORE POWERFUL THAN MY CIRCUMSTANCES

76

Use "I Am" Statements

Remind yourself, "I am more powerful than my circumstances." "I am here to make a difference." "I am a coffee bean."

HOW TO BE A COFFEE BEAN

77

Have a Windshield Mentality

There's a reason why your windshield is bigger than your rearview mirror. You are meant to look forward more often than you look back, and you are meant to utilize more space to see where you are going and less space to see where you've already been.

HOW TO BE A COFFEE BEAN

78

Be Humble and Hungry

Humility is essential to being a coffee bean. Always be willing to learn from everyone you meet. Never think you know it all. Look for ways to learn and grow. Always strive to get better. Be hungry with a passion to take action.

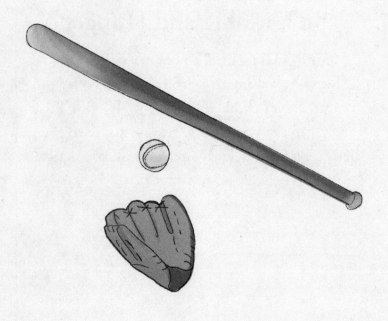

HOW TO BE A COFFEE BEAN

79

Make the Next Opportunity Great

Many call the game of baseball a game of failure because even a great hitter will fail two out of three times. Yet every at bat represents an opportunity to make the next one great. It's the same with life. You may have had a bad day yesterday, but today represents a new opportunity to make it great.

159

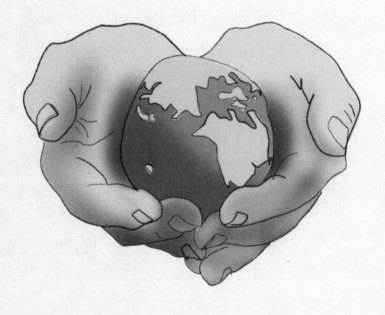

160

HOW TO BE A COFFEE BEAN

80

Make Life a Mission Trip

Don't just have a mission statement. Don't just have a mission in your mind. Be on a mission to make an impact. Life consists of a yearly trip around the sun—make it a mission trip to make a difference.

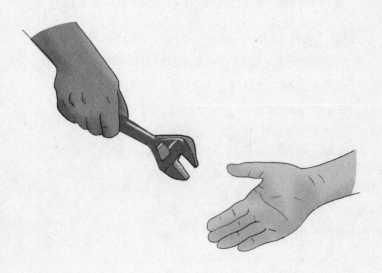

162

HOW TO BE A COFFEE BEAN

81

Look to Be Useful

A person looking to be useful will always find
people who need help and will benefit them
in the process. Intentional positive impact in
another human life is one of the greatest ways to
show gratitude for the blessings in yours. Look
for ways to be useful to others each day.

163

HOW TO BE A COFFEE BEAN

82

Don't Overthink

It's easy to allow overthinking to get in the way of overcoming. You can only have one thought and experience at a time. So slow down and turn clutter into clarity. Instead of thinking of all the ways it won't work out, think clearly about what actions you can take that will make things work.

166

HOW TO BE A COFFEE BEAN

83

Keep Getting Up

In life, no one keeps track of your wins and losses. They will, however, pay attention to those times you don't get back up after getting knocked down. Pick yourself up, don't quit, and keep getting up every time you get knocked down. The world will be better because you didn't give up.

HOW TO BE A COFFEE BEAN

84

Be a Truth Seeker

Don't make up your mind about something
before understanding all sides of the story
and all information regarding the debate.
Now more than ever, be a critical thinker
and a truth seeker.

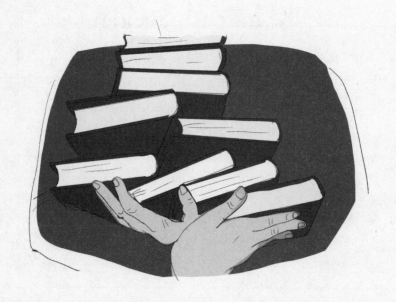

HOW TO BE A COFFEE BEAN

85

Be a Lifelong Student

Realize that life is a university, and everyone is a teacher who teaches us how to do something either the wrong way or the correct way. Learn from everyone you meet. Learn from those you follow on social media. Learn from successes and mistakes, and you will grow exponentially.

HOW TO BE A COFFEE BEAN

Pay It Forward

Find ways each day to pay forward the blessings in your life. It's easy to do too. Just look for people in need.

HOW TO BE A COFFEE BEAN

87

Have No Enemies

This does not mean you will not be someone's enemy. It means that you won't consider anyone your enemy. You choose daily no longer to carry around resentments and hate for others.

HOW TO BE A COFFEE BEAN

88

Face Your Fears

Most fears aren't real. It's why they say fear is a liar. Fear will lie to you in order to keep you from moving toward your destiny. Don't believe the lies that fear tells. Face your fears and watch as they run away like a barking dog. The dog and fear seem powerful, but they aren't. When you face your fears, you realize you are more powerful than they are.

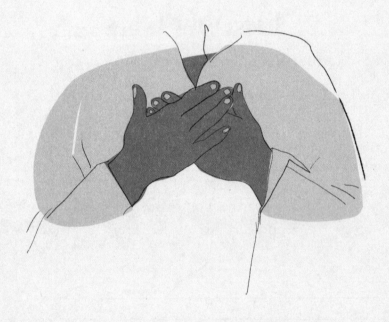

HOW TO BE A COFFEE BEAN

89

Stay Calm When Communicating

Contrary to what some people may think, or the news may have you believe, screaming your thoughts is not always the best way to get your point across and be heard. Don't argue. Don't yell. Slow down, stay calm, and speak with conviction. This actually makes the other person concentrate more to hear what you are saying.

HOW TO BE A COFFEE BEAN

Laugh at Yourself

Don't take yourself too seriously. The ability to laugh at yourself (self-deprecation) will keep you humble and less stressed. It also gives others permission to laugh with you, not at you.

181

HOW TO BE A COFFEE BEAN

Read Books

Reading is how you exercise your mind. Find books that interest you, and commit to reading a little each day. Remember, leaders are readers.

See the BEST in people

HOW TO BE A COFFEE BEAN

92

See the Best in People

Too many judge others based on their worst days, while seeing themselves based on their best intentions. They see the worst in others, not the best. The key to being a coffee bean is to see the best in others. Find the best in them. Look for their good attributes and bring out the best in them.

HOW TO BE A COFFEE BEAN

93

See Potential, Not Limitations

Don't focus on where someone is in their life based on their circumstances or limitations. Instead, look at their potential and see what they can become. What could this person become if they developed their strengths and had the love and support of a coffee bean like you?

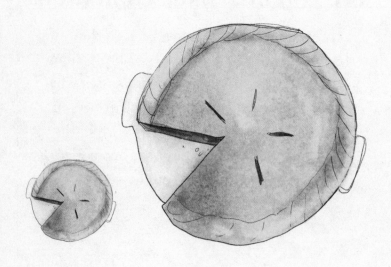

HOW TO BE A COFFEE BEAN

94

Have an Abundant Mindset

Many focus on getting their piece of the pie. They believe that if you are successful, it means they won't be. Or they believe that for them to win, someone must lose. But the key to life is to believe there is more than enough for everyone. Instead of getting your piece of the pie, make the pie bigger for everyone. You can celebrate the successes of others while creating your own success as well.

HOW TO BE A COFFEE BEAN

Tell Me Something Good

When you see someone, ask them to tell you
something good. Then ask them what's not
good so they have an opportunity to be real.
Then ask them how we can make it good so they
remember their power to create positive change.

HOW TO BE A COFFEE BEAN

Be a Hero

Heroes and victims both get knocked down.
But the hero gets back up, and armed with
optimism and belief, they transform their
struggle into victory. Their test becomes a
triumph and a testimony to share with others
so that they can become heroes as well.

HOW TO BE A COFFEE BEAN

Have Only Good Days

Having a bad day is a choice. At any time of the day, you can stop a bad day and start it over and make it a good day. It doesn't matter if it's 9:00 a.m. or 9:00 p.m. You get to choose what kind of day you want to have.

HOW TO BE A COFFEE BEAN

Be You

There's no one like you. You are unique.
You are special. No one has your eyes and your
fingerprints. Don't try to be like anyone else.
Just be you, and each day become a better you.
Always remember that an original is more
valuable than a replica.

198

HOW TO BE A COFFEE BEAN

99

Meet People Where They Are

Everyone is going through something. Don't expect them to be happy or positive or energetic like you. Meet them where they are. Seek to understand them. Listen to them. Empathize with them. Once you meet them where they are, you can lift them up and help take them where they need to be.

199

"BE *present*"

HOW TO BE A COFFEE BEAN

100

Be Present

When people feel seen or heard there is a moistening in the eyes. Yet in 99% of our conversations, this doesn't happen. You can change that. When you're in the presence of other people, put your phone away. Tune out distractions and be present with the person you are with. Give them your full energy and attention.

HOW TO BE A COFFEE BEAN

101

Be Punctual

Be on time and even show up early whenever possible. This shows that you respect other people's time and sets the standard for how you want others to value your time.

HOW TO BE A COFFEE BEAN

102

Be Prepared

Ben Franklin famously said, "When you fail to prepare, you prepare to fail." When you prepare, you are more likely to succeed. Preparing gives you confidence. Preparing helps you perform better. Preparing leads to great knowledge and understanding. Be prepared and little things will turn into big accomplishments.

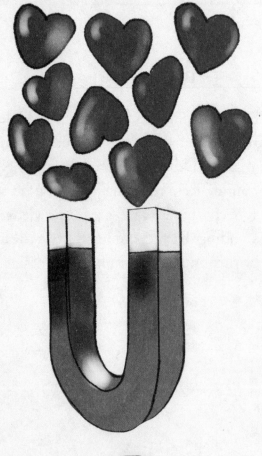

HOW TO BE A COFFEE BEAN

Become a Love Magnet

Everyone is looking for love. When you become love, then guess what?! Everyone will be looking for you. When you become a source of love, you will attract more people and love to you. Love yourself. Love others. Receive the love that comes back to you.

HOW TO BE A COFFEE BEAN

104

Rise above Your Circumstances

Remember that your circumstances have no power over you. One day you are in traffic, and it bothers you. The next day you're in a great mood, but the same traffic doesn't bother you. It's not the traffic. It's not the event. It's always your state of mind. Rise above your circumstances with a positive state of mind.

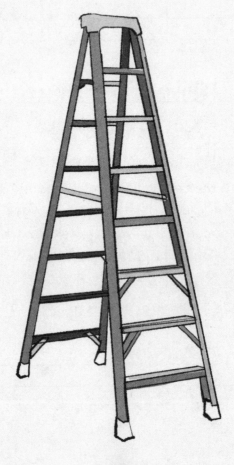

210

HOW TO BE A COFFEE BEAN

105

Remember Where
You Came From

Most people who had to work and struggle their way to the top have a distinct humility and character about them. They remember where they came from, who helped them along the way, and the sacrifices they've made. As a result, they continue to work hard, rise up, and help others rise as well.

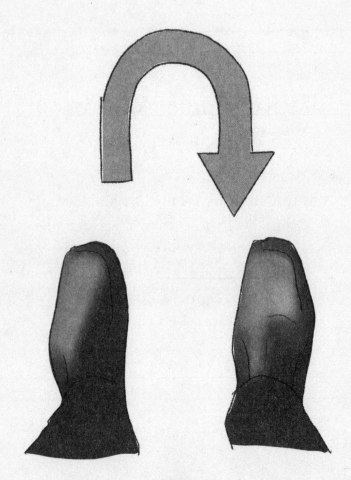

212

HOW TO BE A COFFEE BEAN

106

Believe People Can Change

We (the authors of this book) know people can change because we changed. When you believe people can change for the better, you will work to help them. You will also root for people to be successful because you know that successful people help others become successful.

213

I WILL <u>NOT</u>

LET <u>ANYONE</u>

Walk

THROUGH MY MIND

with their DiRty FEET

AND NEITHER

<u>SHOULD YOU.</u>

— Gandhi —

107

Don't Let Critics into Your Head and Don't Let Praise Go to Your Head

What people think of you is none of your business. Gandhi said, "I will not let anyone walk through my mind with their dirty feet," and neither should you. Nowadays with social media, you will have more fans and critics than ever. Don't focus on what people say. Just keep showing up, doing the work, getting better, and making an impact.

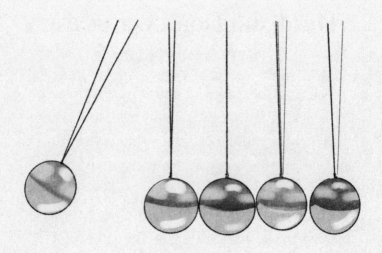

HOW TO BE A COFFEE BEAN

108

Keep Your Vision Alive

Despite the circumstances, regardless of the setbacks, no matter the obstacles, and even through the success, maintain momentum toward your vision. Keep your vision alive and it will keep your momentum moving forward.

Give yourself Credit

HOW TO BE A COFFEE BEAN

109

Give Yourself Credit

Think about what you have overcome in your life so far. Think about the perseverance, grit, and strength it took to be where you are right now. Even if you are not where you want to be, you can celebrate how far you have come. You are braver, bolder, and stronger than you give yourself credit for.

220

HOW TO BE A COFFEE BEAN

110

Take the High Road

Don't lower yourself by engaging in the traffic of busyness, stress, drama, fighting, and senseless arguments that distract and divide. Choose to elevate yourself and take the high road where there's less traffic and more peace, purpose, and joy.

HOW TO BE A COFFEE BEAN

111

Finish Strong

In everything you do, finish strong. Finish by sprinting across the finish line. Finish with nothing left in your tank because you gave your all. Finish each day knowing you gave your best. Finish with no regrets.

223

Other Books by Jon Gordon

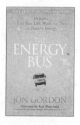

The Energy Bus

A man whose life and career are in shambles learns from a unique bus driver and set of passengers how to overcome adversity. Enjoy an enlightening ride of positive energy that is improving the way leaders lead, employees work, and teams function.

www.TheEnergyBus.com

The No Complaining Rule

Follow a vice president of human resources who must save herself and her company from ruin and discover proven principles and an actionable plan to win the battle against individual and organizational negativity.

www.NoComplainingRule.com

Training Camp

This inspirational story about a small guy with a big heart, and a special coach who guides him on a quest for excellence, reveals the 11 winning habits that separate the best individuals and teams from the rest.

www.TrainingCamp11.com

The Shark and the Goldfish

Delightfully illustrated, this quick read is packed with tips and strategies on how to respond to challenges beyond your control in order to thrive during waves of change.

www.SharkandGoldfish.com

Soup

The newly appointed CEO of a popular soup company is brought in to reinvigorate the brand and bring success back to a company that has fallen on hard times. Through her journey, discover the key ingredients to unite, engage, and inspire teams to create a culture of greatness.

www.Soup11.com

The Seed

Go on a quest for the meaning and passion behind work with Josh, an up-and-comer at his company who is disenchanted with his job. Through Josh's cross-country journey, you'll find surprising new sources of wisdom and inspiration in your own business and life.

www.Seed11.com

One Word

One Word is a simple concept that delivers powerful life change! This quick read will inspire you to simplify your life and work by focusing on just one word for this year. *One Word* creates clarity, power, passion, and life-change. When you find your word, live it, and share it, your life will become more rewarding and exciting than ever.

www.getoneword.com

The Positive Dog

We all have two dogs inside of us. One dog is positive, happy, optimistic, and hopeful. The other dog is negative, mad, pessimistic, and fearful. These two dogs often fight inside us, but guess who wins? The one you feed the most. *The Positive Dog* is an inspiring story that not only reveals the strategies and benefits of being positive, but also an essential truth: being positive doesn't just make you better; it makes everyone around you better.

www.feedthepositivedog.com

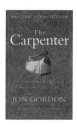

The Carpenter

The Carpenter is Jon Gordon's most inspiring book yet—filled with powerful lessons and success strategies. Michael wakes up in the hospital with a bandage on his head and fear in his heart after collapsing during a morning jog. When Michael finds out the man who saved his life is a carpenter, he visits him and quickly learns that he is more than just a carpenter; he is also a builder of lives, careers, people, and teams. In this journey, you will learn timeless principles to help you stand out, excel, and make an impact on people and the world.

www.carpenter11.com

The Hard Hat

A true story about Cornell lacrosse player George Boiardi, *The Hard Hat* is an unforgettable book about a selfless, loyal, joyful, hard-working, competitive, and compassionate leader and teammate, the impact he had on his team and program, and the lessons we can learn from him. This inspirational story will teach you how to build a great team and be the best teammate you can be.

www.hardhat21.com

You Win in the Locker Room First

Based on the extraordinary experiences of NFL Coach Mike Smith and leadership expert Jon Gordon, *You Win in the Locker Room First* offers a rare, behind-the-scenes look at one of the most pressure-packed leadership jobs on the planet, and what leaders can learn from these experiences in order to build their own winning teams.

www.wininthelockerroom.com

227

Life Word

Life Word reveals a simple, powerful tool to help you identify the word that will inspire you to live your best life while leaving your greatest legacy. In the process, you'll discover your why, which will help show you how to live with a renewed sense of power, purpose, and passion.

www.getoneword.com/lifeword

The Power of Positive Leadership

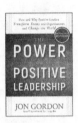

The Power of Positive Leadership is your personal coach for becoming the leader your people deserve. Jon Gordon gathers insights from his bestselling fables to bring you the definitive guide to positive leadership. Difficult times call for leaders who are up to the challenge. Results are the by-product of your culture, teamwork, vision, talent, innovation, execution, and commitment. This book shows you how to bring it all together to become a powerfully positive leader.

www.powerofpositiveleadership.com

The Power of a Positive Team

In *The Power of a Positive Team*, Jon Gordon draws on his unique team-building experience, as well as conversations with some of the greatest teams in history, to provide an essential framework of proven practices to empower teams to work together more effectively and achieve superior results.

www.PowerOfAPositiveTeam.com

228

The Coffee Bean

From bestselling author Jon Gordon and rising star Damon West comes *The Coffee Bean*: an illustrated fable that teaches readers how to transform their environment, overcome challenges, and create positive change.

www.coffeebeanbook.com

Stay Positive

Fuel yourself and others with positive energy—inspirational quotes and encouraging messages to live by from bestselling author, Jon Gordon. Keep this little book by your side, read from it each day, and feed your mind, body, and soul with the power of positivity.

www.StayPositiveBook.com

The Garden

The Garden is an enlightening and encouraging fable that helps readers overcome the 5 D's (doubt, distortion, discouragement, distractions, and division) in order to find more peace, focus, connection, and happiness. Jon tells a story of teenage twins who, through the help of a neighbor and his special garden, find ancient wisdom, life-changing lessons, and practical strategies to overcome the fear, anxiety, and stress in their lives.

www.readthegarden.com

Relationship Grit

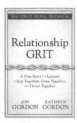

Bestselling author Jon Gordon is back with another life-affirming book. This time, he teams up with Kathryn Gordon, his wife of 23 years, for a look at what it takes to build strong relationships. In *Relationship Grit*, the Gordons reveal what brought them together, what kept them together through difficult times, and what continues to sustain their love and passion for one another to this day.

www.relationshipgritbook.com

Stick Together

From bestselling author Jon Gordon and coauthor Kate Leavell, *Stick Together* delivers a crucial message about the power of belief, ownership, connection, love, inclusion, consistency, and hope. The authors guide individuals and teams on an inspiring journey to show them how to persevere through challenges, overcome obstacles, and create success together.

www.sticktogetherbook.com

Row the Boat

In *Row the Boat*, Minnesota Golden Gophers Head Coach P.J. Fleck and bestselling author Jon Gordon deliver an inspiring message about what you can achieve when you approach life with a never-give-up philosophy. The book shows you how to choose enthusiasm and optimism as your guiding lights instead of being defined by circumstances and events outside of your control.

www.rowtheboatbook.com

230

The Sale

In *The Sale*, bestselling author Jon Gordon and rising star Alex Demczak deliver an invaluable lesson about what matters most in life and work and how to achieve it. The book teaches four lessons about integrity in order to create lasting success.

www.thesalebook.com

The One Word Journal

In *The One Word Journal*, bestselling authors Jon Gordon, Dan Britton, and Jimmy Page deliver a powerful new approach to simplifying and transforming your life and business. You'll learn how to access the core of your intention every week of the year as you explore 52 weekly lessons, principles, and wins that unleash the power of your One Word.

The Energy Bus for Kids

The illustrated children's adaptation of the bestselling book, *The Energy Bus* tells the story of George, who, with the help of his school bus driver, Joy, learns that if he believes in himself, he'll find the strength to overcome any challenge. His journey teaches kids how to overcome negativity, bullies, and everyday challenges to be their best.

www.EnergyBusKids.com

Thank You and Good Night

Thank You and Good Night is a beautifully illustrated book that shares the heart of gratitude. Jon Gordon takes a little boy and girl on a fun-filled journey from one perfect moonlit night to the next. During their adventurous days and nights, the children explore the people, places, and things they are thankful for.

The Hard Hat for Kids

The Hard Hat for Kids is an illustrated guide to teamwork. Adapted from the bestseller *The Hard Hat*, this uplifting story presents practical insights and life-changing lessons that are immediately applicable to everyday situations, giving kids—and adults—a new outlook on cooperation, friendship, and the selfless nature of true teamwork.

www.HardHatforKids.com

One Word for Kids

If you could choose only one word to help you have your best year ever, what would it be? *Love? Fun? Believe? Brave?* It's probably different for each person. How you find your word is just as important as the word itself. And once you know your word, what do you do with it? In *One Word for Kids*, bestselling author Jon Gordon—along with coauthors Dan Britton and Jimmy Page—asks these questions to children and adults of all ages, teaching an important life lesson in the process.

www.getoneword.com/kids

HOW TO BE A COFFEE BEAN

The Coffee Bean for Kids

From the bestselling authors of *The Coffee Bean*, inspire and encourage children with this transformative tale of personal strength. Perfect for parents, teachers, and children who wish to overcome negativity and challenging situations, *The Coffee Bean for Kids* teaches readers about the potential that each one of us has to lead, influence, and make a positive impact on others and the world.

www.coffeebeankidsbook.com

Other Books by Damon West

The Change Agent

The Change Agent tells the true story of a well-raised kid, three-year starting quarterback, and a young person filled with potential . . . until a shocking addiction took hold. Armed with a program of recovery, a renewed faith, and a miraculous second chance at life, Damon emerged from more than seven years of prison a changed man. His story of redemption continues to inspire audiences today.

The Locker Room

An indispensable exploration of some of the most critical and most difficult issues faced by professionals, coaches, athletes, and students today, *The Locker Room* is a must-read resource that belongs in the libraries of anyone who seeks a life or culture that can not only overcome adversity, but can also use it to reach their goals and improve their communities.

The Locker Room Playbook

In *The Locker Room Playbook*, bestselling authors Damon West and Stephen Mackey teach you how to apply the principles and concepts found in *The Locker Room*. You'll find lists of core lessons, chapter summaries, detailed lesson breakdowns, discussion questions, exercises, and key takeaways in every chapter.

234

The Coffee Bean for Kids

Perfect for parents, teachers, and children who wish to overcome negativity and challenging situations, *The Coffee Bean for Kids* teaches readers about the potential that each one of us has to lead, influence, and make a positive impact on others and the world.

www.coffeebeankidsbook.com

235